CW01651978

Bridge Street (above): A row of fifteenth and sixteenth century houses which mark the northern boundary of the town.

(left): The end wall of the red house shows an example of brick noggin. This is the infilling of the space between the beams of a house with bricks - not the usual plaster.

The Eight Bells (right): This late sixteenth century range of buildings shows the clay tile roof over four restored oriel windows on the first floor. The central doorway is the original sixteenth century entrance.

The
Eight
Bells

Youth Hostel: This was a late fifteenth century home and shop which in the nineteenth century was one of the maltings in the town. The sack hoist in the roof v
used to haul sacks of barley to the first floor to be malted.

Close: This is a fine Tudor house with a lovely seventeenth century spider window. In the nineteenth century it was the home of Francis Gibson (1805-1858) created Bridge End Garden and built the Fry Art Gallery.

ON AVI·MATRISQUE ELIZABETH P FRY HAN

Castle Street & Fry Art Gallery Interior (above and left):
Some of the fine fifteenth and sixteenth century timber framed buildings you will find in this street. Most of the windows are eighteenth or nineteenth century additions.

Bridge End Garden (far left):
Francis Gibson created this garden as a series of seven interlocking spaces. The Dutch garden (bottom right) is a copy of the style made popular by William III and Mary II in the 1680s. The Summerhouse was built between 1837-1840 and has lovely interiors by Lewis Fry in memory of his grandfather Francis Gibson and his mother Elizabeth.

Castle (above):
The remains of the twelfth century castle keep are still impressive today – especially when you realise you are looking at the cellar level of the castle. There was a ba within the keep in the eighteenth century and the smal tower was added in the 1790s as a signalling post in th event of a French invasion.

Museum (left):
The Museum, opened in 1835, was one of the first purpose built museums in the country. It houses artefac from all around the world as well as much of more loc interest.

Church Street / Museum Street (above):
The junction dates from the thirteenth century but the shops are fifteenth and sixteenth century only with later windows.

Church Street / High Street (right):
Further along Church Street you find this Cambridge gault brick nineteenth century shop with splendid corner windows.

Corn Exchange (left):
The Corn Exchange was designed in an Italianate style in 1847 by Richard Tress and is now the library.

(above):
In the centre of the Market Place is a drinking fountain in the High Victorian Gothic style. It was designed by John Bentley and was a gift to the town from the Gibson family to celebrate the marriage of the Prince of Wales to Princess Alexandra of Denmark in 1863. It is decorated with scenes from the life of Moses (see detail above).

Saffron Walden has had a market since 1141. Market days are Tuesday and Saturday now.

Barclays Bank (above):
Barclays Bank, which dominates the Market Place, was designed by Eden Nesfield in 1874 in a neo-Tudor style for the Quaker bankers, Gibson & Co.

Town Hall (left):
The neo-Tudor style is continued in the stone arched and timber framed portico which was added to the existing Town Hall building in 1879 when George Stacey Gibson was Mayor of Saffron Walden. It was designed by Edward Burgess.

(above left):
The town's coat of arms forms a pun on the name of the town with saffron crocuses "walled in". This has been in use since 1549.

Church of St. Mary the Virgin

The Parish Church of St Mary the Virgin is the largest parish church in Essex and reflects the wealth of the town at the time of its building between 1470 and 1525.

(above):

The Banner of the Most Noble Order of the Garter is that of R.A. Butler, M for Saffron Walden for 36 years, who grave is at the east end of the church yard.

(right):

The nave ends in this spectacular chancel screen given to the church b William Tuke in 1923 in memory of h wife. The Rood figures on it were added in 1951 in his memory.

(left):

The tower is fifteenth century with th spire designed by Thomas Rickman ir 1832. The clock dates to 1823 and has Westminster chimes from 8am to 10pm only!

Cross Street

(above):
This marks the beginning of the Rows – the Medieval and Tudor shopping centre. Fine Tudor shop windows can be seen on the blue shop.

(left):
The Cross Keys Hotel clearly shows where the roof was raised in the eighteenth century above the early timber framed elements of the building.

'old Street

ıbove):
·olphin House is a sixteenth century house which used to be one of the many pubs in ıe town. You can see the decorated bressumer beam picked out in black against the ;nk paint, as is the sign of the plaster work Dolphin.

'ight):
ːarly sixteenth century timber-framed house in Gold Street, now divided into two.

Abbey Lane

In Abbey Lane, which once led to Walden Abbey, you can find both the United Reformed Church and the Almshouses.

(left):

The United Reformed Church has a lovely Regency portico with Ionic pillars and a classically simple facade and is one of many non-conformist chapels in the town.

(below):

The Almshouses were originally founded in 1400 as The Guild of our Lady of Pity. On the dissolution of religious guilds in the 1550 it was refounded as Edward VI Almshouses. The presen buildings date to 1834. This area is also the site of the original Saxon settlement.

igh Street
bove):

uakers have met in the town to worship since the 1650s. is Meeting House was rebuilt in 1879 to accommodate e pupils from the Friends' School which moved to the wn in that year.

ight):

the top of the High Street stands the Baptist Church nich was rebuilt in 1879 to replace the original 1774 ilding.

e War Memorial was dedicated in May 1921 to the 158 en from the town who died in World War I. Since then 3 more names have been added, 51 from World War II, e man who died in Palestine and one man who died in orthern Ireland.

Friends' School
(above): Friends' School was founde
Croydon in 1702. Following an outbr
of illness, new premises were sought
George Stacey Gibson gave the land
new school to be built. It was designe
by Edward Burgess and the school m
in 1879. The school has the longest
unbroken history of all the Quaker
schools in Britain.

Teacher Training College
(left): The Teacher Training College
funded by George Stacey Gibson w
gifts of both land and money. It ope
in 1884 and closed in 1978 when it
became a language school which, i
turn, closed in June 2007.

ıdley End House

ıce the site of Walden Abbey, Audley End House is the
maining portion of a Jacobean home built by Thomas
oward, 1st Earl of Suffolk, and completed in 1614. The
ounds were laid out by Capability Brown in the 1760s - he
dened the River Cam to form the impression of a lake in front
the house. Cricket has been played on the front lawns since
e 1840s.

rd Braybrooke, whose family once lived at Audley End
ouse, runs a miniature railway through teddybear-filled
oodlands and over the Cam with both steam and electric
comotives.

The Common

The Drinking Fountain at the top The Common was built to commemorate the Golden Jubilee of Queen Victoria in 1887 and w opened by the Mayor Joseph Bell on 20th June 1887. The avenue o trees was planted by Saffron Walden Town Council in 1980 with Common Beech, London Plane, Turkey Oak and Norway Maple.

(left):

The wonderful display of daffodil was the Rotary Club of Saffron Walden's Millennium project. The bulbs are Virginia Wright variety and were planted by local primar school children.

(Back Cover)

The Turf Labyrinth on the far side of The Common is the largest in the world and certainly dates fron 1699 and very probably has Medieval origins.